THE CHANGING FACES OF

Banbury

BOOK ONE

Brian Little

Robert Boyd
PUBLICATIONS

Published by
Robert Boyd Publications
260 Colwell Drive
Witney, Oxfordshire OX8 7LW

First published 1998

Copyright © Brian Little and
Robert Boyd Publications

ISBN: 1 899536 21 3

07700539

OTHER TITLES IN THE *CHANGING FACES* SERIES

Bladon with Church Hanborough and Long Hanborough
Botley and North Hinksey
Cowley
Cowley: Book Two
Cumnor and Appleton with Farmoor and Eaton
St Clements and East Oxford: Book One
St Clements and East Oxford: Book Two
Eynsham: Book One
Headington: Book One
Headington: Book Two
Jericho: Book One
Littlemore and Sandford
Marston: Book One
Marston: Book Two
North Oxford: Book One
Summertown and Cutteslowe
St Ebbes and St Thomas: Book One
St Ebbes and St Thomas: Book Two
Wolvercote with Wytham and Godstow
Woodstock: Book One
Woodstock: Book Two

FORTHCOMING

Bicester: Book One
Cowley: Book Three
Cowley Works
Eynsham: Book Two
Faringdon and District
Jericho: Book Two
North Oxford: Book Two
Oxford City Centre: Book One
South Oxford
Thame
Witney: Book One
West Oxford

Printed and bound in Great Britain at The Alden Press, Oxford

Contents

Cover illustrations

Front: Bridge Street, 1897. Queen Victoria's Diamond Jubilee.

Back: Banbury Cross, 1860.

Acknowledgements

I would like to thank the following for their help at different stages in the production of this book. I express particular gratitude for help given to Christine Kelly, Curator's Assistant at Banbury Museum, Martin Allitt, Senior Library Assistant in charge of the Banburyshire Study Centre at Banbury Library, and Paul Napier and staff at the Banbury Guardian newspaper. I am also indebted to the following for their help: Cicely Bailey for sharing her memories, Barry Davis for help in identifying photographs, Martin Blinkhorn of Blinkhorns Photography, David Williams, former transport manager at Hunt Edmonds and in particular my sincere thanks must go to Margaret Little, my wife, for kindly word processing the manuscript and offering a sounding board at all times.

I am grateful to the following for permission to reproduce photographs and illustrative material: The Neithrop Association for the Protection of Property and Persons, Simon Townsend (Banbury Museum), Harold Hobbs, Ethel Usher, Charles Hunt, John Dossett Davies, Fred Mason, George Buzzard, Kathleen Hemmings, Maureen Thomas, Susan Cherry, Richard Lay, Keith Manning, Doris Durham, Hazel Haskins, Ella West. Eileen Reed, Christine Bennett, Rowland and Peggy Gilbert, Gwyn Warburton, Graham Wharton (N.O.C.) and Michael Jones.

My thanks are also due to Peter Couchman of the Oxford, Swindon and Gloucester Co-operative Society and to Penny Thomas, Trademarks Manager for Bass P.L.C.

Preface

This book is about the centre of the town. It seeks to identify the people and the processes responsible for the changing character of Banbury. Traditionally, family-run businesses predominated with home life located above the shop. During the last forty years these families have dwindled in number and commerce has become rooted in the multiples. Accommodation above the shop is either for storage or occupation by people who have nothing to do with the retail activities below them.

The sectors are arranged according to the principal streets which collectively form a pattern that has changed little since mediaeval times. In some cases names are not the same. Fish Street is now George Street. A few like Cross Cherwell Street no longer feature on the local map.

1998 is an appropriate year in which to write a book of this kind. Work is due to commence on a new central shopping provision. The outcome will be a polarisation of retail services and huge changes to the urban fabric at the eastern end of the town centre. A further consequence will be the creation of a townscape with distinct old and new areas.

My book is based on a wide range of documentary and photographic resources and, most importantly, on memories arising from a place of work such as Hunt Edmonds Brewery or long term residence in Banbury.

In the sectors which follow I have endeavoured to tease out the essential qualities of the town. Sometimes these become part of the nostalgia of the place. The sight of livestock gathering in the streets for market day sales undoubtedly contributed significantly to the town's Banburyness in the early 1920s. However, many people still come to browse amongst the Thursday produce stalls in the Market Place and certain street names such as Horse Fair and Butchers Row offer a permanent memorial to past trading.

At the moment, my intention is that Volume 2 will be topic based and feature aspects of the town which do not conform to a division into streets and districts.

Introduction

Banbury lies at the heart of an informal region known locally as Banburyshire. This stretches from Edge Hill to Deddington and from roughly Hook Norton towards Brackley. Much of the area is characterised by red soils, warm brown buildings and, in the villages, by a fair proportion of thatched roofs. Present day visitors to the town bring with them a vision of the Cross and of cakeshops but many disperse to Stratford for Shakespeare, to Oxford for dreaming spires and to the Cotswold towns for their nationally acclaimed limestone charm and antique shop image.

The story of Banbury is the tale of how twin Saxon hamlets turned into a mediaeval burgh which the Victorians then expanded and industrialised. Fairs and markets locally date from the twelfth century. In 1138 Alexander, Bishop of Lincoln, granted tolls from Banbury market to Godstow Abbey — a sure sign that the market was flourishing. Street names indicate that the buying and selling of goods was not confined to the Market Place but was happening in parts of the town as widely separated as the Horse and Cow Fairs.

Markets and fairs were inextricably mixed and were essential ingredients in the life patterns of the town. Banbury gathered around the spaces they occupied.

In the days before Bishop Alexander de Blois' Banbury Castle of the twelfth century, there were mills and meadows on the lower ground whilst along the valley sides, open fields of arable were more characteristic.

Although the seventeenth century Civil War and its aftermath left our town without its castle, the Market Place and the part of Banbury stretching westwards to the Cross and Horsefair still contain many traditional elements. These have enabled the town to retain something of its Banburyness in an age of hi-tech and distribution industries. In the words of William Raynor of the *Independent on Sunday,* 'the Cockhorse town gallops on'.

From Bridge Bar to mid-Victorian Town Hall

At the outset of 1998, Bridge Street is a partially blighted part of Banbury. Many businesses on the northern side have closed down or been moved out due to central area redevelopment and there is some evidence of adverse impact on the southern edge. The history of Bridge Street suggests a more important past, especially as far as retailing and industry are concerned. Mediaeval Banbury had this street as part of its core area.

In Victorian and Edwardian times, the Cow Fair (Town Hall) end of this street was a very busy part of the town on market day. As the pictures show, there were waggons and carts, drovers and farmers as well as numerous cows.

Until about 1980, family businesses flourished and people lived above their shops. A familiar trader from just before the Second World War was F.J. Mason, the butcher, at No. 60. In 1938 he took over the building from Andrews transport business. Drivers had been accommodated on the premises and parking for the vehicles secured within the yard of the Catherine Wheel (south side opposite the Town Hall).

F.J. Mason enjoyed a fifty years association with the Banbury Stockyard and received a decanter in recognition of this milestone. Right up until 1988 he bought livestock to generate his own supply of well hung meat.

In the late 1930s, most of this meat went to the carriers from the villages but thereafter the majority of the customers were from the Cherwell streets area or from the ranks of the many farmers who came to Banbury on Thursdays. Bulk purchasers, especially after the war, were schools and hotels.

Top: Premises of F.J. Mason, butcher.
Centre and bottom: Inside the premises.

Within a short distance, and on the same side of the road, was the bakery and cafe of Arthur Wincott. The bakehouse was in Mill Lane but the cafe faced Bridge Street and was visited by many of those whose bus journeys began and ended in Bridge Street.

Wincott's shop.

Right: Advertisement for Wincott's café.
Below: Wincott's market stall.

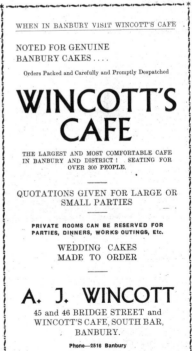

WHEN IN BANBURY VISIT WINCOTT'S CAFE

NOTED FOR GENUINE
BANBURY CAKES . . . .

Orders Packed and Carefully and Promptly Despatched

WINCOTT'S CAFE

THE LARGEST AND MOST COMFORTABLE CAFE
IN BANBURY AND DISTRICT !   SEATING FOR
OVER 300 PEOPLE.

QUOTATIONS GIVEN FOR LARGE OR
SMALL PARTIES

PRIVATE ROOMS CAN BE RESERVED FOR
PARTIES, DINNERS, WORKS OUTINGS, Etc.

WEDDING CAKES
MADE TO ORDER

A. J. WINCOTT

45 and 46 BRIDGE STREET and
WINCOTT'S CAFE, SOUTH BAR,
BANBURY.

Phone—2516 Banbury

There were several specialities at Wincotts, not least the cakes iced and decorated by Kay Kent, and like the family of Betts before them, they claimed that their version of the Banbury cake was the genuine one. Beyond Wincotts were Butlers the fruiterers who were agents for the Oddfellows Friendly Society.

E. E. CLUFF

Specialist in Children's, Ladies' and Gentlemen's

Boots and Shoes

KEEN VALUES

Our Stocks include the following well-known brands :—

GIPSY QUEEN	UNOME	DIANA
GIPSY KING	DRY FOOT	DIANIC

LARGE STOCKS OF LEATHER AND GRINDERY

BRIDGE STREET   ::   BANBURY

Advertisement for Cluff's footware business.

Until the 1960s, another name of distinction was Jimmy Cluff whose footwear business had been handed down by his father. Earlier in the century the firm had made its own shoes using hides tanned in a workshop close to the Strugglers, a Mill Lane public house with canal connections. When the stockroom was finally cleared, boxes of tiny shoes were discovered. These has been destined for sheep as a protection against footrot.

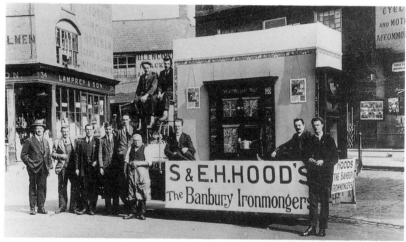

Hood's float. Left to right standing: E. Dutton (Manager), customer, C. Bond (driver), J. Painsbury, L. Brooks (assistant), G. Peachey (warehouseman), C. Gill (commercial traveller), F. Stanley (later Manager), P. Miller.

If ever a shop merited the title 'emporium' it was Hoods before modernisation. Its labyrinthine character ensured that you could buy anything from a nail to a roll of chicken wire but also that you never got to meet all those who worked for this family-run ironmongery. As the photograph shows, the original owners were S and E. H. Hood from whom the business was purchased by Mr. Orchard who lived next door in Marston House. Management then passed on through a succession of people: Dutton, Stanley, Baylis until finally the Jakemans acquired and still run the firm. An employee of Hoods, with many years experience there, is Vera Baylis. Born in Castle Street, she first worked for *Morland's Advertiser* newspaper. Her memories of Hoods are varied and extensive.

Hood's premises today, still on the same site but redeveloped.

Unlike some other Banbury shops, the firm kept gentleman's hours, 8.00 a.m. to 5.30 p.m. Monday to Friday and 8.00 a.m. to 6.00 p.m. on Saturday. They were observors of Tuesday half-day closing and indeed Eric Jones, a shop assistant, played football for the town's early closers. Two of Vera's colleagues were Arthur Coleman and a Mr. C. Gill. Arthur started in 1936 as an errand boy (age 14) with a bicycle. He was succeeded in the job by George Haynes. Both before and after the war, Arthur worked in the warehouse. Gill was the commercial traveller. He visited shops and farmers in and beyond the villages.

In 1980, E. W. Hobbs added his personal memories of Hoods in a letter to the *Banbury Guardian.* His working life began in 1923 with a seven year apprenticeship. At age 15 he earned 5s. (25p) a week delivering goods by hand cart and also taking items to the carriers carts on Thursdays and Saturdays. Even to the present day the tool room of the shop has a desk bearing his name as well as that of Len Brooks.

Over the years Hood's trade has benefitted in some curious ways. One has been a steady demand for coffin effects notably shrouds and brass plates and handles. Another way is to do with Banbury Fair. In the past owners of rides came in for paraffin as well as nuts and bolts. One year prizes were purchased for a particular stall.

In fulfilling more regular demands, Hoods delivery van has played a vital role, enabling the firm to reach customers as far away as Chipping Norton and Eydon.

Back in the shop and during the days when Miss Stanley ran the office as many as half a dozen people were required. Today with computers no one is full-time on that side of the business.

Hoods was large enough to have a social organisation. In common with many other firms there were staff summer outings especially to seaside resorts such as Bournemouth and Brighton. At Christmas, a dinner and dance took place usually at the Crown Hotel for which Ken Prewer and his band played.

In the 1920s and 1930s, the street was characterised by the number of small family run businesses. Stantons, owned by an Adderbury/Twyford family, prided themselves on their personal service; Austins a ladies outfitter was noted for beautiful gowns; A.J. Butler sold fruit and vegetables — Mr. Butler was a former Mayor of Banbury; Allsopps, on the Crown side, sold prams, toys, children's items and furniture; Trolleys had a noted pork pie business and cooked the pies in their cellar which gave off wonderful smells as you passed by. George Dawson, an auxiliary fireman, had a varied business. This ranged over cold meats and confectionery with a small restaurant at the back. He also did some baking and his hot cross buns at 7 for 6d were amongst the best in town. George started work at 5.30 a.m. to get the buns out. In addition a number of houses had adapted a small front room to sell sweets.

The south side of the street also included some notable local businesses, contemporaries of Mason and Wincott. There was Miss Sirmon with her cake shop and cafe, Willis a jeweller, and Caves who were furniture removers.

Established over a Century.

Telegrams: Telephone:
"Cave, Contractor, Banbury"   Banbury 2498

William Cave

(Mrs. F. E. Cave)

Railway Parcels Cartage Agents

Household Removals and Warehousing

★ ★ ★

BRIDGE STREET · BANBURY

Oxfordshire

A remarkable wartime example of the Cave enterprise was that countless service personnel, who were heading for the railway station, paid over 6d. so that their bicycles could be stored in Cave's yard. The business also handled parcels which came by train and also acted as the Midland Red bus office. As has already been indicated some of the activities used to happen behind the Bridge Street frontage. Typical was the making of sports shirts to the rear of a jewellers and approached by way of an alley.

Life for those who lived in the street could be exciting from time to time but also occasionally noisy. Once a year there was an ox-roast on the Thursday of the Fair week. The last of these was in the Crown yard in 1956.

For a short period just after 1945, the Fair amusements extended to the bridge. Then, as now, a great commotion accompanied the arrival and departure of the rides and shows, and above all there was the sight of Mr. Wilson with his hat and whip personally supervising movements.

A peaceful crowd outside the Town Hall.

The space outside the Town Hall saw many gatherings of people, usually for occasions such as the announcement of election results or a Royal Proclamation. Not all were as peaceful as that pictured. At the election of 30th April 1859 when Sir Charles Douglas won the seat from Bernard Samuelson, the *Banbury Guardian* reports that fighting was more or less continuous in the Market place from 2.00 p.m. onwards. Neither candidate was present for the announcement of the result which the mayor was prevented from making by a volley of eggs. The victorious candidate took refuge in the Red Lion Hotel, later making good his escape through a back window. This did not prevent the crowd from burning his effigy in the High Street. Later, a number of men who worked at Samuelson's Britannia works were charged with a series of public order offences.

In the background of the photograph, the line of shops, some with their awnings down, give an indication of busier times for Bridge Street. On the extreme left was Stanton's grocery store. This was always a very clean shop and had the additional function as agent for parcels carried by the Oxford Bus Company.

At the back of the crowd is a bus stop for the Midland Red Company whose local and village services started from the Cow Fair in front of the Town Hall. Their local office was at 33 Bridge Street.

Four years prior to the issue of this advertisement, Berry Austin became a conductor with the company. He received a blue uniform but had to provide a rack for tickets. Each conductor made his own, usually by invading Hoods of Bridge Street for a suitable piece of wood and a supply of springs from mouse traps so that the blocks of tickets could be held in place. Company timetables were available in booklet form for 3d. Disposal of 12 copies meant 3d. commission for a conductor.

Midland Red Bus Company.

Frederick W. Dunkin was a general printer in Bridge Street. He was well known as a Methodist local preacher and did all the printing work for his church. This included items such as anniversary sheets. Unlike many retailers, Dunkin was responsible for his own advertising. From a very striking box display we learn that his work embraced reports, memoranda, note headings, balance sheets, memorial cards, programmes and bill heads. His slogan was, 'If you like the book, try the printer!'

Left: Frederick W. Dunkin.
Below left: A Waverley Hotel advertisement.
Below right: Cadbury Memorial Hall painted sign for hot and cold baths.

The "Waverley"

Commercial Temperance Hotel,

BANBURY.

Close to Great Western, and London and North Western Railway Stations.

⋅∻⦾∻⋅ ⋅∻⦾∻⋅

Accommodation
Homely and Comfortable.

⋅∻⦾∻⋅ ⋅∻⦾∻⋅

Hot and Cold Baths.

⋅∻⦾∻⋅ ⋅∻⦾∻⋅

GOOD STABLING.
Charges very moderate.

T. DUMBLETON, *Proprietor.*

At the close of the nineteenth century, Mr. J. Dumbleton became associated with the temperance hotel movement. Previously, great coaching inns such as the White and Red Lion Hotels (see High Street section) had dominated the market for visitors. The Waverley Hotel and Restaurant catered for 18 guests who were able to enjoy the facilities of hot and cold baths. By 1920, this institution had turned into the Bluebird and incorporated a café. A regular bus service ran between it and Middleton Cheney. Known as the yellow buses, this company was owned by a Mr. Charles.

The picture shows an attractive building on the same site as today's National Westminster Bank. In the doorway of his shop is Jack Leach, son of Rocky. The premises were adjacent to the Town Hall and marked the western extreme of Bridge Street. Like his father, Jack made rock but also sold cigarettes and tobacco. The most likely date of this photo is the late 1920s/early 1930s. Jack had a later trading position and that was facing the Oxford Road between St. John's Street and the Mount.

It is impossible to mention everyone who traded in the centre of the town. However, a place must be found for Gardiners who baked a Banbury cake but were also famous within the town and area for their dough cakes.

Jack Leach outside his shop.

The present Barclay's Bank building.

The present Barclays Bank on the corner of Bridge Street and Broad Street was developed on the site of the Old George. This inn had been very popular with farmers and drovers on market days but located in a part of Banbury where the public house was a predominant building.

As this photograph of Barclays suggests, there was created a landmark building. It was designed to harmonize with its surroundings, especially in the almost total use of Hornton stone. A corner entrance set back slightly meant a considerable street widening improvement to Broad Street.

These premises were constructed to replace the Cornhill Bank which had been sited on Castle gardens land. This land had cost Edward Towerzy £40 in 1703. Such was the gain in value that, when the building was conveyed to Richard Woodfield in 1757, the price was £245. At that time the premises were in the occupation of Elisha Heydon, a mercer, who was probably one of the original partners in the bank firm of Bignell, Heydon and Wyatt. In 1822, the baking activity was purchased by Joseph Gibbins and Joseph Ashby Gillett. Up to the time of the amalagation with Barclays in 1919, one or more members of the Gillett family had always been partners.

Once again it had been demonstrated that for Banbury physical change of location and design was matched by significant social change in ownership and responsibility.

In 1987, a Mrs. Kenyon was interviewed concerning her memories of the Old George public house when run by her grandmother. Different cutomers frequented different parts. The snug was used by regulars such as bank managers whereas drivers and so called rougher men were accommodated in another section. The entrance to the inn was cobbled and at the rear were stables where Mrs. Kenyon's father kept a horse and lots of dogs. Amongst her most vivid memories was the arrival of the dray horses with the barrels of beer from which ale had to be drawn off in quart jugs. During the First World War her grandmother cooked for the van loads of soldiers who drew up periodically.

The Old George public house.

Hunt Edmunds Brewery

An industrial company which came to play a dominant role not only in Bridge Street but also in the wider Banbury area was the brewery business of Hunt Edmunds. (24: advert for 1951)

Introducing . . .

The Drink of the Year

Banbury
Festival Ale

ON SALE IN ALL
OUR LICENSED HOUSES

Hunt Edmunds & Co. Ltd.

Hitchman & Co. Ltd.

THE BREWERY

BANBURY   CHIPPING NORTON

Advertisement from 1951.

Thomas Hunt.

Hunt Edmonds and Co. Ltd. was founded by Thomas Hunt who had previously farmed at Cropredy. In 1807 he purchased the Unicorn Inn in Banbury's market place and, for ten shillings, conveyed it to his son John Hunt of Upper Boddington (a plumber and glazier).

Rusher's Directory for the town tells us that a John Hunt was at the Unicorn from 1832 to 1841, but was also a Market Place maltster 1835 to 1839 and a maltster and brewer in Bridge Street at the time of the 1841 census. Thomas and John Hunt junior then formed a partnership but this had been dissolved by 1848. By now there were three buildings within the business: the Unicorn, a Bridge Street brewhouse, and a malthouse in Parson's Meadow Lane (towards the George Street end).

Williams Edmunds.

Further partnerships followed, notably that with William Edmunds in 1850. Together they expanded the premises over the period to 1866 but a more fundamental issue was water supply for beer making. This was solved in the mid-1860s by acquiring springs and shallow wells in the Green Lane area.

By 1886, the company had two breweries and 64 'tied' public houses in Banbury. Also about this time bottling began on a small scale.

Until 1913, most deliveries from the brewery were achieved by horse drawn drays. The first motor lorry arrived in 1913 and from 1914 to 1917 there was a steam wagon available. The First World War had a significant effect on the company, especially in the way that female workers ap-peared for the first time in the office, the bottled beer department and the wine and spirits cellar. In February 1965, the bottling department benefitted hugely from the installation of a carbon dioxide plant. It meant that beer could be pumped without resorting to air pressure.

Ladies crating bottled beer.

In 1918, Hunt Edmunds lost the services of one of its Directors, Ernest Stephen Holland. He died aged 34 not as a result of war action, but arising from a fall at his Chipping Warden home, 'The Gables', where, with his brother and co-director, he used to entertain touring Australian cricket teams.

Ernest Stephen Holland

Dunnell and Sons' advertisement from 1890.

THE OLD BREWERY, BANBURY.

---•••---

DUNNELL & SONS,

Brewers & Spirit Merchants.

---•••---

Price List of Ales and Stout.

	Brand on Cask.	Per Barl. (36 galls.)	Per Kild. (18 galls.)	Per Firk. (9 galls.)	Per Pin. (5 galls.)	Cost per gall.
East India Pale Ale	EIPA	54/-	27/-	13/6	7/6	1/6
India Pale Ale	IPA	48/-	24/-	12/-	6/8	1/4
*Pale Ale	PA	36/-	18/-	9/-	5/-	1/-
No. 1 Strong Ale	XXXX	48/-	24/-	12/-	6/8	1/4
,, 2 Superior Mild Ale ..	XXX	42/-	21/-	10/6	5/10	1/2
,, 3 Mild Ale..	XX	36/-	18/-	9/-	5/-	1/-
,, 4 Ditto, ditto	X	30/-	15/-	7/6	4/2	-/10
,, 5 Ditto, ditto	T	24/-	12/-	6/-	3/4	-/8
Double Stout	DS	48/-	24/-	12/-	6/3	1/4
Single ditto	S	36/-	18/-	9/-	5/-	1/-

* *Light Dinner Ale, especially recommended for Family use.*

---‡---

Good Haymaking and Harvest Ales at 6d. and 4d. per gallon.

---‡---

CARRIAGE PAID.

The same year the business expanded yet again with the acquisition of Dunnell's North Bar brewery which, in 1998, is the site of a car park. Over the next three years, a new name appeared at the top of the company, R. H. A. Holbech. He lived at Farnborough Hall (now owned by the National Trust) and was a member of a well-known Warwickshire family whose name became associated with the children's ward at the Horton Hospital.

Bernard Tims operating the bottling machine.

Les Sims of Kings Sutton checking the stock.

Despite the depression in the 1930s, bottling grew in importance and new tied houses were added. These included the Easington in 1929 (at first called the Springfield) and the Crown, close to the brewery, which by 1935 had become a commercial hotel. Company Christmas parties came to be held there though with mixed fortunes. At first everything was free and company guests drank the place dry. Later, vouchers were issued which entitled the holder to free starter drinks, and company employees were allowed an overnight stay if this was felt to be desirable!

The Easington Hotel.

Established 1615.   Re-modelled 1931

Appointed by the A.A., R.A.C., H.R.A., c.V.M.

CROWN HOTEL

FREDK. W. DULLINGHAM, Proprietor

Spacious New **Ball Room** (with Conservatory Lounge).
Family and Commercial—Special Commercial Rates.
Central Heating and H. & C.
Running Water in Every Room.
Parties of Every Description Catered For.
Banquets, Wedding Receptions, etc.
Everything Up-to-date at Popular Prices.
Ten Lock-up Garages.

BRIDGE STREET :: BANBURY

Phone : 259711 Banbury. Grams : Crown Hotel, Banbury

Advertisement for the Crown Hotel, 1938.

In the years after 1945 and until the brewery closure, Hunt Edmunds was run on somewhat military lines by senior staff with army backgrounds. Despite this regimentation, the company employed some remarkable personalities.

Robert D'Oly Aplin was the head brewer. He was a very quiet man from the local family of solicitors. Encounters with him near his office often revealed a beer on the desk and a black labrador under it.

Company secretary was Leslie Crowder whose swivel chair afforded a view of the town hall which he would face when trying to make a point. His paper work revolved around the theory that, given time, some problems solved themselves.

Fred Hobbs was bottling manager and second to D'Oly Aplin. He gained a special reputation for the way in which he bottled the Guiness. Many of the women in his department hailed from Grimsbury.

Another notable at the brewery was general handyman Albert Coleman. Sadly, he had difficulty in walking, possibly because of encounters with dray horses! One of Albert's tasks was to clean the car of Lance Harman, the managing director. The outcome was not always synonymous with success, partly because of bird activity in the chestnut tree beneath which the car was parked, and partly because, on at least one occasion, he used the wrong cleaning fluid and took the colour out of the paint.

A much more mysterious person was the man in the old malthouse who was on the payroll yet appeared to do nothing all day other than polish nails. Those who worked as draymen were very proud of their work which was done within delivery teams which changed daily. Sheets issued by the transport manager told them where they would be working the next day. Great care was needed to get the balance right. Two of the transport workers were sons of barge owners and could not read or write. On one occasion, working together, they got deliveries so mixed up that these had to be completely redone on the following day.

Lance Harman (right) opening a Licensed Victuallers' Garden Party at Denham in 1968.

Someone who gave a lifetime of service to the firm was Alf Hone. He worked as a young lad in the bottle room, then with the horses and finally on the lorries. Alf and his distribution mates had memories of very old cabs with no heating. The lorry crew's day could be very long, especially at Christmas when the rush was on: 7.30 a.m. to 9.30 p.m. was not unusual.

The malthouse was another part of the brewery that had long service employees. Reg Adams was foreman maltster for 48 years. He made himself responsible for the early stages of the beer-making process.

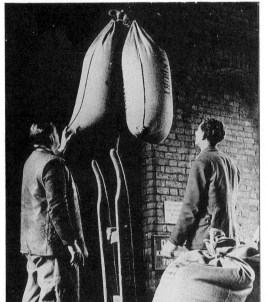

Grain handling. Left: Reg Franklin, on the left, receives the sacks of barley. Below left: turning the barley during the malting process. Below right: inspecting the malted barley.

Hunt Edmunds' staff outing to London. The photograph includes Fred Jones; Works Manager; Raymond Miller, Company Secretary; Lance Harman, later to become Chairman; Col. Maurice Edmunds, Chairman; Thomas Langley Jones, Brewer and Director; Frederick Matthews, Director; Percy Goodwin, Manager at Chipping Norton; George Edmonds, Brewer; Mr Barnes, Manager at Witney; Arthur Sproule, Manager →

Wines and Spirits; Mr Hall, Manager at Worcester; Bill Berry, Tied House Accounts; Jack Goodway, Accountant; Ron Letts, Accountant; Ted Wilson, Manager Delivery Department; Arthur Coombes, Accountant; Beryl Kimberley (née Watts), Secretary to Mr Miller; Phil Clare, Manager at Evesham; Maurice Angell, Works Department; Hazel Haskin (née Frost), Secretary to Mr Harman; John Bolton and Eric Bolton.

In the prevailing workforce structure it was inevitable that there would be husband and wife partnerships. Jack Walton was a member of the barrel washing team whilst his wife Mary did noble service in the staff canteen. The Waltons were so much a part of the company that they lived in a cottage in the brewery yard.

Socially, and through the activities of the company sports club, there appears to have been other bonds which contribute to many happy memories of Hunt Edmunds.

There were staff outings to London, events through the social club and annual reunions. The soccer season 1963-64 saw the first ever brewery side in Banbury league football. After an uncertain start they finished a worthy eighth, no mean feat in view of the lack of a home ground. The cricket fixtures went back to at least the early days of the century and ranged from matches against town sides such as Brackley to company teams like Collissons.

Brewery float in the Carnival Procession, June 1953.

The secrets of a successful brewery appeared as a pamphlet from Hunt Edmunds Ltd. at the Banbury Industrial Exhibition in April 1951. In this the brewers made a very telling statement, the company 'has a tall chimney and a big heart'. When the chimney came crashing down in 1972, that heart ceased to beat and brewing could no longer be accounted a lone survivor of market town skills in Banbury. The business was acquired by Bass Mitchell and Butler in 1965 together with 187 public houses.

A view of the brewery site showing the chimney.

Broad Street
Home of Co-opville

The Banbury Co-operative Industrial Society was born in 1866. Its first shop, which was for groceries and provisions only, was located in Bridge Street. It was much used by families from the Cherwell industrial quarter of the town where there were thriving companies such as Samuelsons and Barrows. Wives from this area welcomed a form of retailing more in tune with their working class needs and attitudes.

Co-operative Society trade grew rapidly and just two and a half years later the move to Broad Street took place.

The first Co-op shop.

Frederick Lamb

Frederick Lamb was secretary and manager from 1878 to 1894. The development of departments owed much to his guidance and experience gained from years in London. His premature death in 1894 was a blow to the movement.

Former Co-op premises, now a row of side street shops.

A steam mill was erected in Broad Street in 1881. It used an engine and boiler supplied by Barrows at a cost of £369 10s. A warehouse for grain and flour was added two years later.

The flour mill.

Bread making and confectionary followed closely in the wake of farming and milling. The bakery shown in the picture was erected in 1903, enlarged four years later and improved in 1915. By this last date profits had reached in excess of £10,000.

The central bakery.

Deliveries became a feature of Co-op business before the turn of the century and these included both coal and milk.

An early coal lorry.

The milk premises in Lower Cherwell Street.

In 1947 and for one day only, milk had to be pasteurised at Oxford instead of Banbury. This was due to severe flooding in Lower Cherwell Street.

Records of the annual accounts in the early 20th century show that the various departments were doing well. Grocery and Provisions for instance recorded a profit of just under £700.

The Banbury Co-operative and Industrial Society half-yearly report and balance sheet for September 1952 indicates that deliveries of goods inside and outside Banbury were still important. Emphasis was on van distribution but as the picture shows this was not always the case. The village in the photograph is Milcombe where a horse waits quietly in front of delivery cart number 38. The *Oxford Mail* for 28th October 1964 recorded the retirement, at the age of 23, of the last of the milk delivery horses. Called Prince, he had given 16 years of service when finally he headed the last ever cart. Prince was retired to the Society's rest home for horses at Ningwood on the Isle of Wight.

Delivery by horse and cart at Milcombe.

Branch stores in the villages appeared from 1868 onwards and developed out of an increasing awareness by agricultural labourers of how the Co-operative movement could help their rural plight.

The opportunity for new development in Banbury arose from the demolition of an old inn, the Coachsmiths' Arms, which had been on the corner of Broad Street and Fish Street (now George Street). Here, Mr. Allen's design was translated into bricks and mortar by Kimberley and Son of Banbury at a cost of £3,516. This was one of many examples of Kimberley's work in the town. Their yard and offices were in Britannia Road and were demolished in March 1998 to make way for retirement flats.

Much rejoicing greeted the opening of the new Co-op building in 1908. Selections of music were played by bands on the flat roof.

The Co-op premises opened in 1908.

W.M. Lickorish, Managing Secretary.

In 1916, W. M. Lickorish summed up the spirit of enthusiasm in town and county for the Co-operative Movement when he said that what matters is 'the essential faith in the better instincts of the human heart to work for their security as a driving force in the achievement of the race.'

By this date, Broad Street was lined with Society-owned buildings selling all essential needs including meat which owed much to a slaughterhouse and piggeries on the Hightown Road Estate.

The Broad Street drapery and furnishing premises.

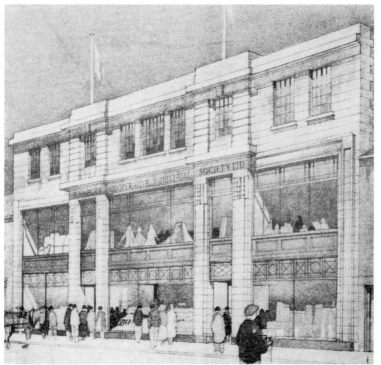

The Arcade Building.

A major change in the face of Broad Street came about in 1934 with the construction of an arcade building. This was a miniature Selfridges for an early 1930 small town.

Part of the crowd at the opening of the Arcade.

At 3.00 p.m. on 10th March 1934, and in front of a huge crowd that completely filled the town centre end of Broad Street, Mr Lickorish opened the Arcade building, which had three levels, and ushered in a new phase in the history of Banbury Co-opville. Mr Lickorish remarked 'a long-cherished dream has at last been realised!' In a letter to the *Banbury Guardian* published on 9th April 1998, Pauline Grain, Mr. Lickorish's granddaughter, of Poole, Dorset, recalls how proud her grandfather was at that time to have the honour of opening the premises.

She recalls treasured memories of her grandfather and notes his railway family origin. He left Grimsbury Wesleyan School at the age of thirteen to become a railway clerk. After only a few months in this position, he joined the Banbury Co-operative Society. He studied at evening classes and with the aid of correspondence courses until he was thirty to enable him to progress in the business, eventually becoming a chartered secretary.

Later on the same day, members of the General and Educational Committees (see opposite page) attended an official tea and then a grand concert given by the Banbury Co-operative choir and string orchestra.

The Arcade.

Central to the Arcade was a glass dome which offered a pleasing effect under artificial lighting conditions. Departments at this level included outfitting, footwear and hairdressing for men whilst female interests were served by a drapery, ladies' footwear and hairdressing.

Mr. F. WALTON
(General Committee)

Mr. J. W. BONHAM
(Treasurer)

Mr. A. W. LINES
(Educational Committee)

Mr. W. F. HAYDEN
(General Committee)

Mr. S. J. HARRAP
(Educational Committee)

The
General and Educational
Committees

At the Opening of the Central Arcade Building, March, 1934

Mr. J. BRIDGES
(General Committee)

Mr. W. J. TRINDER
(Educational Committee)

Mr. R. MARTIN
(General Committee)

Mr. P. WILLIAMS
(Educational Committee)

Mr. W. G. MASCORD
(General Committee)

Mrs. B. HERBERT
(Educational Committee)

Mr. I. C. THOMAS
(General Committee)

Mr. E. A. PHILLPOTTS
(Assistant Secretary)

Mr. C. BARNETT
(Educational Committee)

The Cosy Café on the first floor served 'dainty' teas and light refreshments.

The top floor of the building was reached by lift or staircase and was reserved for office and administration purposes.

The corridor in the offices. In the picture are the general offices where steel revolving pass book safes had been installed.

Someone who missed the excitement of the Arcade's coming was Henry James Cooke J. P. (seen on the left). He had been General Manager of the Society but died in 1931, just a few days after the annual 'mystery outing'. A wide cross-section of Banbury society attended his funeral which inspired an acknowledging letter to the company magazine *Wheatsheaf* penned from the family home in Newland Road.

H.J. Cooke, J.P. (seated) with W.H. Lickorish.

A grocery department entry in a C.W.S. window display competition.

In November 1949, the Banbury Guardian newspaper recorded yet another first occasion for the Co-operative Movement. This was the conversion of the grocery shop into Banbury's first "help-yourself" store. Two early visitors to the new style provision were Mrs. Jeffs and Mrs, Bailey and they were shown the layout by Miss Smith of Grimsbury.

Luke Coleman (left) and his shop at Adderbury (right).

Luke Coleman was manager of the Broad Street grocery operation from 1927 until his retirement in 1965. His career with the Co-operative Society was a long one with periods spent at Bloxham, Leamington (part of the Banbury organisation) and Adderbury. Luke devoted most of his life to retailing, the only exception being a brief spell at Townsend Nurseries soon after leaving school at the age of 14.

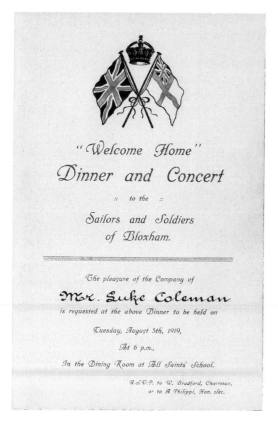

Luke was still serving in the forces when a 'Welcome Home' Dinner and Concert was held for the men from Bloxham who had served in the Army and Navy. Those, like Luke, who were unable to attend received a parcel and an invitation card which they could save as a souvenir.

Luke Coleman's invitation to the 'Welcome Home' Dinner and Concert.

The Co-op often entered a Float in fete processions such as the Hospital one.

The Banbury Co-operative Society was a pioneering organisation in another sense. In 1921, a large garage with archway entrance was built. At that time it was the only building of size in the town and so the space was used for everything from boxing matches to old people's teas.

Dean's newsagents at
No. 6 Broad Street.

A Broad Street personality unconnected with the Co-operative Society was Tommy Dean whose death was reported in the local press in 1984. In his way he was a Banbury legend. A short way into Broad Street from the High Street end, Deans had a flourishing newspaper business at a time when papers made up for a lack of other means of getting information.

Thomas Dean was probably meant to be a newsagent. He was one of nine children all of whom were brought up to do an early morning paper round. The family home was in Shotteswell and the move to Broad Street came about 1924. At first, Tommy sold papers across the counter of the Fleur de Lys where Granny Dean was mine host. His shop was a mere stone's throw away at No. 6. When he took over the premises there was an unmistakable appearance with the front entrance resembling a stable. Indeed, Molly Adams, the previous occupant, had a habit of looking over it.

No. 6 Broad Street developed into the Dean family home with nine living above the shop. On the Bridge Street side of the front door was a passage which led behind the newsagent's to some houses and ultimately to the yard of the Catherine Wheel.

Dean developed a thriving business which included sweets and tobacco as well as papers and magazines. His customers were located in every part of the town but there was always a special place in his heart for people living in the Cherwell Streets area and the Great Western Railway properties off Hightown Road. These people never owed money. Grimsbury was another big area for him and comprised two substantial rounds. Tommy used to cycle to the Horton Hospital with the papers where he was the agent for newspaper supply over a period of 50 years.

Left, Tommy Dean waiting to serve and, right, relaxing in his garden.

Saturdays were special. He used to stock the *Oxford Mail* as well as the *London Standard* and *London Evening News*. With the aid of his own printing machine he stop pressed the football results which were so eagerly awaited that his paper queue stretched from the shop to way past Barclays Bank. Tommy collected his papers from the railway station which is where he also sold the *Birmingham Argus* to his Grimsbury customers, especially to save the extra journey to the shop.

At the height of his business, Dean utilised the services of 16 delivery boys. One of these was Dermot Gallagher, currently Banbury's own Premiership League football referee.

Dean's shop, like so many family businesses, had a wider social role during World War II. He allowed bicycles of service personel to be left in the yard and shed whilst they went to film shows at the Grand Cinema.

At the level of the family, the layout of No. 6 was a subtle mixture of opportunity and constraint. There was space for a few flowers, two fruit trees with land for a few chicken as well as two pigs in a sty. Against this, the family relied on an outdoor toilet.

When Banbury Borough Council introduced a buses only scheme for Bridge Street, which meant that people from Grimsbury could only access Dean's shop by using a combination of Cherwell Street and George Street, it proved a deterent and severely curtailed Tommy Dean's trade from streets to the east of the railway.

A photograph of Samuelson's men.

This photograph was taken in the 1870s. It includes a man called Gardner (behind the boy on the low stool) whose Broad Street fish and chip shop, taken over from someone called Charles, was another of the few activities not Co-op inspired. The premises had a distinctive layout. Customers had to walk through a long passage to reach the actual frying area. In doing so they passed a different part where the potatoes were cut into chips.

The Grand Theatre manager.

The Grand Theatre opened on 18th July 1911 and was heralded as 'one of the most attractive theatres in the country'.

Stage productions as well as films were a feature of Grand days. These included concerts. One in particular was especially notable. It was given by children of the Cherwell Infants School in June 1921. Those who paid from ninepence to two shillings and fourpence to see the concert would have been gratified to know that proceeds were going to the Horton Infirmary and Banbury Nursing Association. Patron for the event was the mayor, Sidney James Mawle whose family ran an ironmongery in the High Street.

After 57 years of existence, the Grand showed its last film in 1968. No longer would eager youngsters queue along the length of Pepper Alley so as to guarantee themselves two hours of films which inevitably included Laurel and Hardy. In their place came a different generation of bingo enthusiasts. Next to the Grand Cinema was Woodhull's greengrocery. One tradition which benefitted his trade was the purchase of tomatoes to go with a few rashers of bacon obtained from Butlers in the High.

Broad Street used to boast a saddler called Haynes. Sadly, his son turned into an itinerant and sold shoelaces about the town. Many of the other small shops in Broad Street were approached down steps. A good example was Maris which sold everything.

The Market Place

Despite the historic importance of many of the buildings that surround this space, the Market Place is probably best known for its produce markets and fairs.

In this early photograph of Banbury's Market Place, carts and motor cars are outnumbered by people.

Rocky Leach at his stall.

Compared with today's Thursday and Saturday markets, those of the 1920s and 1930s had more personalities. Rocky Leach was one of these. He was a large man, renowned for his Banbury rock which he made available in a wide range of flavours and colours. Inevitably the cut up sticks of rock caught the attention of a host of insects as well as the children. Much of his time was spent fending off young hands.

Like several other traders, Rocky's market business was tied to a retail shop. Members of the Leach family ran enterprises in different parts of the town, notably Jack Leach in a building behind the Town Hall now replaced by the National Westminster Bank (see Bridge Street).

Also confectioners in the 1920s with two shops and a market stall were Salmon and Catch. These had gone by the early 1960s. Salmon and Catch were both wholesale and retail confectioners. The wholesale activity was dependent on carriers with carts to get consignments of sweets to village shops. They made a proportion of their sweets in North Bar, which is where Violet Beale worked for two years from the age of 14. A colleague especially remembered was Dolly Rutter who hand made chocolates individually.

Violet's starting wage was 10 shillings (50p) a week. Even after a year she was only getting 12 shillings (60p). Mr Salmon maintained that he gave his staff free bags of sweets as a perk of the job. At the age of 23, Violet was on 25 shillings (£1.25) a week and this was for amazingly versatile work. Included in this was the expectation that she would keep the accounts for the wholesale business and produce typed lists of debtors.

Violet was 16 when first she became involved with the firm's market stall. This stayed open to 5.30 p.m. on Thursdays and 9.30 p.m. on Saturdays to catch people going into the last house at the Palace Cinema.

Violet got to know several other market traders including Jack Spencer. On one occasion she was invited by him to go to the market stall holders dance in Leicester. She remembers travelling in Mr Salmon's two-seater car with a dickie behind. Sid Hartwell drove them to the East Midlands.

Jack Spencer was also known to all. His pitch dated from the 1920s and he travelled from Leicester to find buyers for stockings, socks and underwear. In 1945 he moved to Banbury and remained local until his death aged 93.

Competitors in the underwear business were the Peacocks who were also from the Midlands. They had a large square stall offering work to several local girls.

Walker's Stores.

Mr Legge, who was an assistant at Walker's Store in the Cornhill part of the Market Place (circa 1903), had a well-known biscuit business and kept his stall in a stable at the rear of the Angel, a nearby inn. His trade fell victim to the arrival in the early 1930s of F.W. Woolworth, the High Street 3d and 6d store. Biscuits were very much on their agenda.

The inter-war produce market was characterised by longer trading hours, possibly because the town did not empty after work. From 10.00 a.m. to 9.00 p.m. (winter) and 10.00 a.m. to 10.00 p.m. (summer) was not uncommon. The Market Place, illuminated by naphtha flames, came alive after dark, attracting crowds looking for a bargain. The market covered much the same area as today but there were no stalls in Cornhill.

Many stallholders later had shops in the town. Maud Woodhull had a big stall for greengroceries near the Banbury Gas Company shop at No. 34 Market Place.

Wyncolls came from Birmingham to Banbury about 1920. They had a stall outside the Picture House exclusively selling bananas. Success in this business prompted the opening of a shop towards the top of Parsons Street. This was expanded but continued good trade led to the family taking over the old Windmill pub in North Bar.

Gascoignes had a fruit and vegetable stall near to the High Street Tchure as well as a shop in Butchers Row. Their produce was home grown.

Fish stalls lined the diagonal way for wheeled traffic. These included the businesses of Truss and Tony Warren. During the rest of the week, Tony did a street round with his dray and attracted trade with his well-known cry of 'Fish alive-o'.

Nash's fish stall was a notable feature of the 1920s produce market. Nash had a retail shop in Fish Street (George Street). His speciality was shellfish. If, at the end of the day, some were unsold, he put them in a wicker basket and toured the public houses with them in search of customers.

Molds of Neithrop were noted for their produce from their market garden. This included boiled beetroot.

A wartime arrival was the W.I. stall.

Certain traders whose shops faced onto the market took advantage of the opportunity for creating a display on the pavement. Nathan, Robins and Broughton and Wilks were familar examples.

Market Place showing goods on the pavement.

The Pig Market was in front of The Angel.

The three photographs on this and the preceding page reflect the market in all its moods. The first in the sequence reveals a near-deserted Market Place. The camera picks out a tiny huddle of stalls at the Butchers' Row corner and a few carts just beyond well-known shops such as Broughton and Wilks.

The second picture is of the 1920s/1930s market with its concentration of stalls in a triangular area at the western end and a diagonal way for carts and cyclists. Some shops have pavement displays.

A third picture reveals wooden pens, probably for pigs, at the east end of the Market Place. Judged by the absence of people the occasion of the cameraman's visit was not a market day.

All these impressions of Banbury Market Place suggest that there had been great changes since the beginning of the century. In 1903, Thomas Ward Boss, librarian at the Mechanics Institute, observed that there was a pool of dirty water through which pickpockets and other disreputable characters were dragged. At the western end there were some antiquated buildings, including the shops of Mrs. Pepples (a hosier) and Thomas Strange (a jeweller). Sets of five steps had to be climbed to reach these shops.

The Market of the present day provides yet another set of contrasts. Thursday and Saturday gatherings of stalls are a far cry from those of inter-war Banbury. Many of the present traders feel that the market has lost much of its charm and bustle. In Great British Market Week, held in August 1997, there was no sign of the lampshade lady who had been ever present for ten years and no one to take the place of Sid or Alfie. Who can forget Alfie's call from the clocks and watches, ''alf price in the sale'.

Two of the present stallholders who have both seen over 30 years of coming to Banbury, can remember earlier starts, greater competition and more casuals hoping for a pitch.

That the Thursday and Saturday markets have survived says much for the determination of traders but also the process whereby people drift into this way of working. Sylvia Snowden became a stallholder by chance. She had been on holiday with her former husband who was in haberdashery. Snapping away he got a taste for photography and went off to be a fashion photographer whilst she went into haberdashery!

Once a Picture Palace, now a bank.

At the east end of the Market Place is the building currently occupied by Midland Bank. The premises were originally built in the mid-nineteenth century as a corn exchange and, before Martin Blinkhorn's grandfather bought it in 1906, it had contained a skating rink. *The Banbury Guardian* carried a report that on the night of Thursday 1st February 1877 a young man named Harvey employed by Mr Railton, a

High Street sadler, broke his leg while 'rinking' at the Corn Exchange. He was taken to the Horton Hospital (opened 1872) where it was discovered he had broken a small bone in his leg.

From 1906 until 1922, when a consortium including Horace Lester took control, three days a week were devoted to silent movies and three to stage shows. A resident orchestra included Tom Hutchings, Sid Moore and Nellie Alcock (piano). Sid was later to become projectionist at the Grand cinema in Broad Street and also played in the Ken Prewer Band.

The Ken Prewer Band. Left to right: Ken Prewer, Nick Nicholson (cello), George Baker (trumpet), Dudley Metcalfe (violin), Jim Fox (drums), Frank Howe (violin), Sid Moore (violin), Albert Jordan (double base), Tom Hutchings (piano), Mr Hicks (M.C.).

Dorothy Blinkhorn who ran the box office at Blinkhorn's Picture house was always accompanied by a dog. When the animal heard the National Anthem at the end of the performance it used to run into the theatre and see what edible items had been left behind. On one occasion, Armistice Day 1918, the audience were told about the cessation of hostilities at which point the National Anthem was played and the dog gleefully roared around the theatre to the great surprise of those there. Dorothy was later in charge of the British restaurant in Marlborough Road.

Jack Bridges was the man who wound on the film. A hobby of his was novelty bicycles which he used to take to local fetes. Bernard Blinkhorn managed the sound effects for the silent movies himself. On one occasion the film required the noise of a landslide. A large metal wheel was constructed inside of which was a steel drum full of rocks. He and Norman Scroxton trundled the wheel back and forth at the rear of the screen. They experimented with a person in the drum in place of the rocks. Unfortunately they could not control the wheel which plunged through the cinema screen much to the alarm of the members of the orchestra on the other side.

Crowds at the Banbury Fair.

As this Morland picture indicates, the occupation of the Market Place by the Michaelmas Fair attracted large numbers of people. Joyce Baker who was born in 1923 and interviewed in the 1980s remarked, 'Banbury Fair was the highlight of the year'. People like her, who had limited financial resources, would forsake holidays for the opportunity to enjoy rides at 1d or 2d a time. Unlike Joyce, some visitors to the fair , and especially on Thursday, travelled considerable distances. Both railway companies issued special Banbury Fair tickets and coaches came in from all the villages and from as far away as Coventry.

Another person who spoke about the fair was Ann Wheeler. She and her father walked from Deddington to Aynho station and then spent all day enjoying the amusements before returning on a 9 o'clock train in the evening.

Ball's sideshow.

Apart from the Bioscope (an early mobile cinema) and travelling circuses, there were sideshows such as that provided by Ball who claimed to offer the best pictures at 3d for adults and 2d for children. While some folk were enjoying the galloping horses or hearing their fortune from Gipsy Rose Lee, for those who were not faint hearted there was the challenge of the boxing ring. Joyce Baker recalled her father's involvement and that he used to win some money for lasting several rounds. For herself there was also the pleasure of taking home some fairing, possibly ribbons or brandy snaps.

This Michaelmas event was first recorded in 1677. The main reason for the importance of this Autumn Fair was the practice of hiring servants.

In Victorian times, people went to Banbury Fair in their best clothes. However, not all were of good intent. Beggars were rife as were those whose occupation was to relieve careless souls of their 'spare' cash.

An eye witness report of 1856 offers a vision of the true fair goers. 'They bought ribbons and shawls, dolls and toys, ate gingerbread and Barley Cake.'

Parsons Street

Directories for Banbury which cover the part of the twentieth century before 1939 suggest that Parsons Street was more important then than today. You could do a total shop there and the only real omission was a bank. There was no shortage of public houses. These included the Wine Vaults with its snugs and the Reindeer, famous for the pre-Civil war Globe Room.

The Wine Vaults.

The Reindeer Inn, on the left.

R. BRUMMITT & SONS,

Importers of Toys and Fancy Goods,

57 PARSONS' STREET, BANBURY.

The Best and Cheapest House for

TOYS. NEW GAMES. DOLLS. RICHTER'S STONE BRICKS.
PURSES. WRITING CASES. ALBUMS.
LINED WORK BASKETS.
PORTMANTEAUX. GLADSTONES. HAND-BAGS.
HANDKERCHIEF BAGS. DRESSING CASES.
CABINET GOODS. ELECTRO-PLATED GOODS.
BAMBOO ART FURNITURE.
And an endless variety of Goods suitable for Birthday or Wedding
Presents.

57 PARSONS' STREET, BANBURY.

WENHAM LAKE AND ROUGH ICE.

ROBERT H. GIBBS,

Fishmonger, ⁂ Herring ⁂ Curer,

FRUITERER,

Poulterer, and Licensed Dealer in Game,

15 PARSONS' STREET, BANBURY.

Fish fresh from Billingsgate Market and the Sea Coast every day.

— ESTABLISHED 1848. —

Advertisements for Brummitt and Sons and R.H. Gibbs.

The premises of R.H. Gibbs. Fish could also be purchased from Truss.

In 1968, the premises which had been E. W. Brown (No. 12) were pulled down as the building was considered to be in a potentially dangerous condition. This was a tragedy for the town as it had always been regarded as the 'Original Cake Shop'.

During the eighteenth century, the White family had the business. Betty White was renowned for her cakes though reports picture her as a querulous person always complaining about the hardness of the times and the increasing cost of ingredients she used in the cakes. When customers remarked that the cakes were smaller she observed that 'there's currants, they be double the price th' used to be, and then there's butter an' sugar, why they be double the price th' was farmerly.'

Of her husband, 'Old Jarvis White', it is said that he was a profane, idle man who used to spend a lot of time leaning over the hatch of his shop door but he did speak well of Betty's cakes. He reckoned they were so light that one day a sparrow entered the shop and made off with a cake.

During the nineteenth century, there were two owners, Samuel Beesley and Mrs. E. W. Brown. The former sold almost 140,000 two-penny cakes in 1840, some going as far away as America and at least one package was sent to Australia. Mrs Brown was a strict Quaker and insisted that only the men did the baking whilst ladies concentrated on icing and pastries. Latterly, E.W. Brown also offered a café service for lunch and tea at their famous 'Cake Shop' and if you enjoyed a Brown's Banbury Cake then pre-war they could be bought at the rate of 6 for 2s. 2d., 12 for 3s. 9d., 24 for 6s. 10d. and 36 for 9s. 10d.

Above: Brown's premises on Parsons Street. Left: The site as it is today.

Close to the top of Parsons Street and nearly opposite Dossett's grocery store was the butcher's business run by William Jeffs and his two straw-hatted sons. Their specialisation was pickled beef and home-made sausages. William presented a very striking figure with his red complexion and always wore a gold watch chain.

W. A. Truss, fresh and fried fish shops.

A few doors below Dossett's, at Nos. 41 and 42, were the businesses owned by W. A. Truss and Sons. William Arthur Truss first started selling fish and poultry in the early 1920s. He bought a shop which combined antiques with Terry's Photographic Studios above it. William sold fish and chips from an adjacent property, No. 42. Today, these are, respectively, an Indian foods store and a computer business.

Nos. 41 and 42 Parsons today.

The layout of the fried fish shop included a trap door which allowed the fish and potatoes to be lowered into a cellar where they were prepared for cooking and then hauled back up. At the rear, separated by a brick wall, was the dark room for Terry's Electric Studios.

Memories of the early days in Parsons Street are inevitably linked to the Depression when work was scarce and there was not much money about. W.A. Truss gave away one ton of potatoes, chipped and fried, to people who felt that they qualified for a free meal. Soon, Parsons Street became very congested and rumour had it that half the local police force was required to keep some sort of order. In all this excitement, the shop door became detached from its hinges. It was not until midnight of the day when William made his offer that all was once again back to normal.

Another fried fish shop was established in the early 1930s at a location where today there is an entrance to the Castle Shopping Centre close to Oxfam and Laura Ashley, No. 42 Market Place, now Poppy's Restaurant.

Fish came in fresh from a variety of port-based companies; cod from Hull, herrings and sprats from Lowestoft and kippers from Buckie in Scotland. Some of the fish was destined for hotels and boarding houses. Pre-war prices reflected the boast of nothing above a shilling; herrings and coley were 4d. per lb. and dry fish 6d. or 7d. per lb.

The necessary ice came all the way by rail from Northampton. The firm had a two-wheeled flat truck for conveying it from the Merton Street station. Occasionally ice was delivered to cutomers for special events such as a summer champagne party, the distance from the shop to the venue being crucial. Too far and the ice had melted by the time of arrival.

All the poultry came in live and had to be killed and prepared on the premises. At Christmas, this involved intensive work and long hours.

In the 1930s, the produce market included two Truss' stalls on a Thursday and one on a Saturday. Harry Harris, who lived in Castle Street, stood at the latter for some 33 years.

The fish stalls were part of a line of positions that stretched diagonally from the Town Hall end to Parsons Street (see Market section). Truss' stalls at Banbury never did as well pre-war as the one in Stratford market where trade was so brisk that seven assistants were required.

Today, there is still a Thursday fish stall outside Marks and Spencer in Banbury bearing the name of Truss despite not being in the family ownership.

Someone who worked in the Parsons Street shop and on a stall was George Buzzard. He retired at the age of 65 but not before he had completed 50 years with the firm.

George Buzzard.

George started, aged 14, as a delivery boy on a bicycle in 1930. The bike was specially adapted for conveying goods and it had a smaller wheel in the front. Part of George's work was to take fish to the Horton Infirmary for Friday meals. This involved carrying eight wooden boxes with a stone of fish in each, a total of 1 cwt.!

Part of Pilsworth's 'Empire'.

Pilsworth's enterprise was the most wide ranging across the span of outfitting, drapery goods and furnishing. Kathleen Hemmings and Maureen Thomas had mothers (Annie and Susan Hayes) who worked for Pilsworths. Their periods of employment there spanned the years 1904 to 1919.

The firm had strong Irish connections and maintained a well-established retail tradition for living above the shop. In this case, Mrs. Pilsworth (née Norah Fullerton) occupied rooms above the shop which was on the Market Place side of the Banbury Guardian offices.

Maureen Thomas's mother also lived above the shop and always said that you got 'good keep' at Pilsworths, though the 1s. 11d. per week pay was hard earned. The shops, which were on both sides of Parsons Street, had no heating and chilblains became a serious problem. As a shop assistant there was a need to be aware of the customer's status. People of note were served in their carriages in the street.

Mr Pilsworth ran a tight domestic ship as well a hugely influential departmental store with its wide range of clothing and accessories. At night time he always locked at 10.00 p.m. and had to be roused if an employee had gone out for the evening and returned late.

His gentlemen's outfitting manager was Billy Cattell whose wife was a Sister at a doctor's surgery in West Bar. Maureen's mother used to have to confront him in bold language if she needed any boxes for storage.

Annie Hayes.

Susan Hayes.

In the 1930s, ladies were equally well catered for at Lingwood and Steele as they were at Pilsworths. Coats and suits could be had for under 40 shillings (£2)

A mid-nineteenth century business that opened at No. 23 Parsons Street was that of the chemist and druggist G.V. Ball. In February 1844 he took a substantial box in the *Banbury Guardian* to inform 'the inhabitants of Banbury and neighbourhood' that he hoped to keep 'drugs, chemicals, etc. of the purest quality'. Ball also promised 'moderate charges and unremitting personal attention'. He went on to assure people that patent medicines would be genuine and indicated that his stock would include items not normally associated with a pharmacy, namely spices, fancy snuffs and cigars. Finally, almost as an afterthought, he promised that every article would be properly labelled.

Some, at least, of Ball's registers of prescriptions still exist as do various papers which suggest that George had constant but maybe unfounded worries about stamp duty.

G. V. BALL

CHEMIST and DRUGGIST
Parsons' Street

Begs respectfully to inform the inhabitants of Banbury and Neighbourhood that he has commenced business as above, and hopes, by keeping Drugs, Chemicals, &c., of the purest quality, moderate charges, and unremitting personal attention, to be favoured with a share of their patronage and support.

—o—

PHYSICIANS' PRESCRIPTIONS AND FAMILY RECIPES DISPENSED WITH THE GREATEST CARE AND ACCURACY.

—o—

Genuine Patent Medicines

—o—

SPICES, FANCY SNUFFS, CIGARS, &c.

—o—

N.B. EVERY ARTICLE PROPERLY LABELLED

Feb., 1844.

1953

Announcing The Opening of Our New Pharmacy

44 BRIDGE STREET, BANBURY

DISPENSING
PHOTOGRAPHIC
VETERINARY
TOILET
PERFUMERY

A. E. FOX & CROSS CHEMISTS

Proprietors: BANBURY CROSS (CHEMIST) LTD.

23 PARSONS STREET - 44 BRIDGE STREET
5 THE HORSE FAIR

Phone 2039 and 3058 Banbury

Advertisements for G. V. Ball and A. E. Fox.

Ball was also known for his philanthropic activity. He gave the town £3,000 so that a public park could be established. The first phase of this 'People's Park' was finally opened by the Mayoress, Mrs. Bloomfield, in 1912.

The pharmacy was taken over from George Ball by Arthur E. Fox in 1893 and 28 years later Arthur Deacon bought the business and moved a second shop from Middleton Road to Bridge Street, both business trading under the name of A.E. Fox.

Deacon was a major figurehead in the town. He served on numerous health and sports committees and enjoyed a spell as Chairman on Banbury Spencer Football Club. Like many business people of his day, council work was an abiding interest culminating in his being mayor 1942–43.

The original home of *The Banbury Guardian* was in this street. It was from No. 51 that William Potts produced his first paper on the 5th April 1838. The impetus was to demonstrate support for the objectives of the Poor Law Amendment Act as the somewhat lengthy title of 'The Guardian or Monthly Poor Law Register for the district comprised in the unions of Banbury, Bicester, Brackley, Chipping Norton, Daventry, Northampton, Shipston, Southam, Stratford-on-Avon, Witney and Woodstock' reflects. The building is now occupied by the Banbury Bags and Baggage shop and the paper is now produced from offices in North Bar.

Published Every Thursday Morning.
Price 2d.

The
Banbury Guardian

The Leading Business Paper.

100*th YEAR OF PUBLICATION.*

Having the largest circulation
in North Oxfordshire and the
adjacent portions of the Coun-
ties of Northampton, Warwick,
Buckingham, Gloucester and
Worcester.

Advertisement and Publishing Office :
51 Parson's St., Banbury

'Phone 2034

Advertisement for *The Banbury Guardian* from 1938.

Near neighbours of *The Banbury Guardian* in 1932 were a hosier by the name of Sidney Frank Powell, Kingerlee Brothers (fancy goods dealers), the London Central Meat Company, and no less than three tabacconists: Chard and Co. at No. 62, William Lees at No. 49 and Mrs. Jane Turbitt at No. 46.

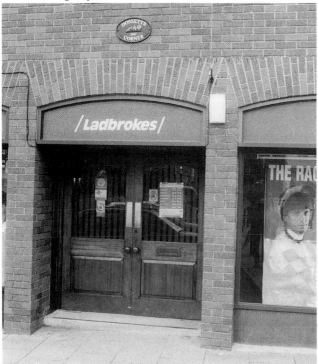

Memories of the corner where Parsons Street and North Bar meet are nearly always dominated by tales of Dossett days. A plaque, 'Dossett's Corner 1887', marks the site of the grocery shop which rivalled Butlers of the High, and commemorates the name still used by many Banburians when talking of that part of the town.

Dossett's Corner at the top of Parsons Street.

Originally, William George Dossett bought the failed business of Frank Hall in 1887. Money for the purchase had to be borrowed from relations and from a man called Vanner but, once up and running, the Dossett enterprise soon gave the impression of stability.

A wine and spirits licence was obtained and this lifted trade into an orbit of contact with big houses like Broughton Castle and Aynho Park. Town people as well as the gentry became customers and there was also a good business to be had supplying village shops. More than thirty such links were established and William George used to collect orders by driving out to the villages in his pony and trap.

W.G. Dossett taken in the Southam Road in 1900.

At first, carriers' carts were used to convey the goods from a nearby warehouse but delivery vans soon followed.

Perhaps the best period for the business was before 1914. The arrival in the town of International Stores as well as Home and Colonial ushered in a period of decline from which Dossett's never really fully recovered. William Dossett died at the age of 84. A measure of the esteem in which he was held can be judged by the presence at his funeral of Mr and Mrs Deacon, Mayor and Mayoress of Banbury.

After William's son had taken over in the early 1940s, he strove to maintain the same high standards. Whenever items were missing from his own stock, a shopping trip to Butler's was considered less humbling than admitting inability to supply. The shop continued under William's name until it closed in 1973 and the building was demolished.

If William and his wife Alice were renowed for the founding of the business, it was their daughter Gertrude who grabbed the society headlines. In a fancy dress parade which was part of a Town Hall Coronation Ball of 26th June 1902, she won a prize for her Bo-Peep costume. The award was made by Councillor Bloxham who was Mayor of Banbury and had organised the event.

Gertrude Dossett as Bo-Peep.

Gertrude features again in a group photograph. Others in the picture are Mabel Dossett, Lottie Carter and Winifred and Ada Hawtin. All the girls came from a family background of trade. George Carter made fizzy water at his North Bar works whilst James Hawtin was a plumber and builder. All the girls went to the Mount School which today is the Banbury House Hotel. On leaving there they moved into a life style which was unhurried and did not expect middle class girls to have careers.

North Bar and
Horse Fair

Before the M40 motorway, the through route for traffic in Banbury was by way of North Bar and Horse Fair. Much of this traffic came from the Coventry direction along what used to be the A423.

In the early days of the motor car, anyone living alongside this road was likely to experience the frustrated motorist short of petrol. Such was the lot of George Pinson and his wife who started their working lives with Stone's Furniture business and who had lived in a cottage in the village of Little Bourton.

The Pinson home at Little Bourton.

In 1912, they bought a property on the main road with the aim of running a chicken farm. However, such were the demands for fuel that, for a while, George cycled into Banbury and returned with cans of fuel. He then realised that the location offered an opportunity for garage services. Two bold notices on the right of the picture announce a 'B.P.' link and urge the motorist to 'Stop Here'.

The Pinson house with garage.

George Pinson with an AA man.

The above phoptograph is a rare example of the work of Terry's Electric Studios which were in Parsons Street. At this stage, pumps have been added to his earlier, more basic garage. Arterial route serving had arrived.

The old St Mary's Church.

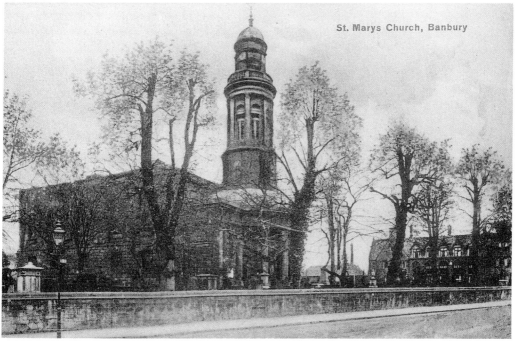

St. Marys Church, Banbury

The new St Mary's Church.

The grandeur of the former building is captured in this early nineteenth century lithograph. It was so revered that the 1798 replacement was greeted with the saying 'Dirty Banbury's proud people built a church without a steeple'.

The new St Mary's was designed by Samuel Pepys Cockerell in the classical style fashionable at the time.

This building demanded appropriate incumbents and they came no finer than the Reverend Lancaster who was vicar between 1815 and 1849. His attire was distinguished by a black coat and waistcoat with pantaloons, black and fitting tight to the skin. Hessian boots reached the knee and there was a small black tassel hanging from the outside of the skin.

A landmark building in the Horse Fair has been Church House dating from 1905. The chief fund raiser for this development was Canon Porter, the then vicar of Banbury.

Porter was an impressive figure. He was a tall man with white hair and sported side-whiskers. Following a leg injury whilst on holiday abroad, he had to use a tall stick. Children especially found him an irritable man who could be intolerant of their slow responses in services.

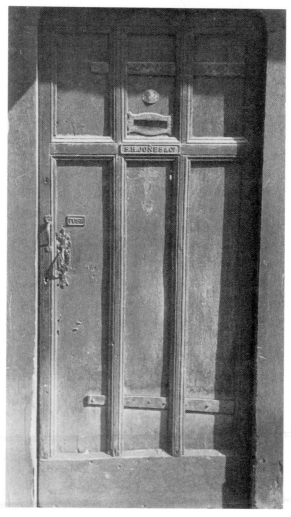

This doorway is from a building pre-dating the Canon Porter Church House. The site was the first home of the fine wines business of S.H. Jones who traded from there until 1901 when the business moved to 62 High Street.

Church House

Church House was home to many theatrical productions both before and after World War II. In April 1939, nine members of Marlborough Road Methodist Church came together in a presentation of 'Passing Brompton Road'. The cast included some well-known Banbury people. There was Albert Chidzy, organist and choirmaster who also ran a music shop in Parsons Street. Randolph Webb who for a time managed the *Banbury Advertiser*, and his wife Winnie who was one of the Morland printing family. Margaret and Richard Paxman were related to the owners of a successful Grimsbury dairy whilst Luke Coleman was manager of the Co-op grocery in Broad Street.

The **BANBURY DRAMATIC SOCIETY** PRESENTS

PASSING BROMPTON ROAD

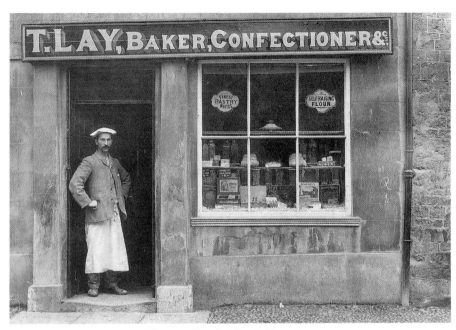

Thomas Lay's North Bar shop.

When Richard Lay closed his bakery business and associated shop opposite St. Mary's Church in the early 1990s, it was the final chapter of bread and cake making by his family. The story began with a bakery in the Old Grimsbury Road and a shop for cakes and teas in Church Lane, Banbury. Thomas Lay was the man behind these initiatives. Harry, his brother, was involved with catering for events such as dances and generated the food from his small bakehouse in Gatteridge Street which was close to Braggins Yard. Thomas moved his business to North Bar in 1907. This shop remained the same until 1952 when Henry Lay had alterations made which created a living room to the left and a shop to the right at the front of the building. Further changes took place between 1968 and 1970 by which time Henry's son Richard had taken over at North Bar.

Harry Lay's shop.

True to its name of Horse Fair, two events established a link with horses though neither has survived until the present day. Throughout the nineteenth century and as late as 1900, Banbury Twelfth Fair was held at the end of January. It lasted four days. The other event was a meeting of the Warwickshire Hunt, often on Boxing Day.

In the years before 1925, hurdles were placed in the Horse Fair every Wednesday evening in readiness for the weekly sheep sales. Some young boys, notably Bernard Blinkhorn, Harold Walker and Tom Hankinson, organised races over the hurdles and often impromptu games of cricket and football were played with a tennis ball in front of Blinkhorn's shop in South Bar.

The George and Dragon stood on the corner of Horse Fair and the High Street. It belonged to Phipps brewery in Northampton and, like several other inns in Banbury, catered for a wide range of customers. A roomy yard was an asset in the age of carriages and carriers' carts. The pre-1914 photograph on the opposite page has a fascinating line of motor cycles. Was this a club outing or merely enthusiasts coming together for the day? A letter to the *Banbury Guardian* some years ago drew attention to the presence of Mr H. Eyre (far left). He had a yeast business in Church Lane. The Banbury Cross branch of Barclays now occupies part of the building. Also in the photograph are Bert Beard (with sidecar in centre), Harry Askew (second right) and 'Doc' Fortescue in the Morgancer on the right.

George Hutchings in his role of town crier.

Another group of people was associated with the Cross at Christmastime. Called the 'Waits', these five men played appropriate music around the town between 4.30 a.m. and 7.30 a.m. In summer their appearance altered to that of a band of minstrels. George Hutchings was one of the five. Well-known as a town crier, George had a typical pose with bell and megaphone. His announcements, ranging from lost property to coming events, were always heard clearly.

The George and Dragon.

The Lady on a White Horse.

Banbury has witnessed many processions, most of which have taken in the Cross and High Street. Some commemorated Jubilees, some unique occasions like the Foresters' gathering in 1907 and some in connection with the Horton Hospital Fete. Invariably a procession included a lady on a white horse, a reminder of the nursery rhyme and possible connection with the Seye and Seles at Broughton Castle (the Fiennes family) since the original lady may have been Celia Fiennes who travelled the highways and byways of this county in the seventeenth century.

South Bar Area

Boy Scouts collecting after the sinking of the Titanic.

The picture is of Boy Scouts from the 1st Banbury Troop. It was taken by Thomas Blinkhorn who purchased his photography business in 1883 from Anthony Beale who had been located at 5 and 6 South Bar from the mid-nineteenth century.

The occasion of this picture was a Scout collection as part of fund raising in connection with the sinking of the Titanic in 1912. Norman Blinkhorn, son of Thomas, is shown on the extreme left. He had started the first Scout group in Banbury only a few years previously. The picture is doubly interesting because the figures around the Cross are draped in black as a mark of respect for those who lost their lives in the disaster.

Norman Blinkhorn.

Beales & Co.,

Every description of Photography . . . undertaken at . . reasonable prices. . PHOTOGRAPHIC ARTISTS,

Children's portraiture a Speciality. . . . . SOUTH BAR, BANBURY.

✱ ✱

Photographic Dealers'

Department.

All kinds of Photographic Apparati, Materials and Roll Films kept in stock.

Developing and Printing for Amateurs.

Dark Room for use of Customers.

Advert for Beale's photographic services.

Ivy Harriss (left) and Gladys Hughes outside Wincott's Café in South Bar.

An all-female event at Wincott's Ballroom.

Number 9 South Bar came to be the other home of the Wincott family. Here, dinners, dances and wedding receptions were held at what was called initially 'The Chocolate Box'. Success necessitated expansion so the neighbouring businesses of Batts and Tyrells were purchased and the name of the expanded business changed to A.J. Wincott. Apart from Christmas Day, the business was open every day including Sundays when the waitresses got 4 shillings (20p) an hour.

The photograph gives a good idea of the scale of the operation. Tea and cakes have been provided for an unidentified all-female organisation.

H.O. Bennett.

Henry Owen Bennett was a prominant professional in the Oxford Road where he lived. A Neithrop Felon for over 50 years, he came originally from Leicestershire in 1913. Bennett began farming at Alkerton but the depression in farming in the early 1920s encouraged him to turn to the textile trade. The purchase of three cottages in the village for £40 enabled him to start the knitwear business. Expansion of this activity encouraged him to open up the St John's Works on St John's Road just off South Bar where he had his base until the early 1940s.

Some of the girls who worked for H.O. Bennett between 1930 and 1935 had followed him from his earlier enterprise and used to cycle to Banbury from as far away as Tysoe.

The girls were very enthusiastic and wanted to make the latest models for the West End trade. These and the range of items from golf coats to woollen cardigans meant that the business was highly successful even if long hours (to 8.00 p.m. each evening) had to be worked.

At the peak of production there were about 100 girls. Closure in 1942 was forced upon Bennett because the Ministry of Labour drafted employees to the Northern Aluminium Company to help boost the war effort. Looking back over some 20 years at the St John's Works, Henry Bennett was able to reflect on a point of contrast with today, he had no women who had returned to work after starting a family.

In the post-war era, the name H.O. Bennett was more closely linked with milk distribution from premises in the North Bar area.

A photograph taken about 1915. Left to right: Fred Mold, Michael Bennett, Jack Turner and Christine Bennett. In front, barely visible, is Donald Gillies.

This picture is important both for the people caught on camera and because of where it was taken. Fred Mold became a teacher at St Mary's School; Michael Bennett and Christine Bennett were both associated with the Wine Vaults, house and Inn, in Parsons Street; Jack Turner ran a fish shop in Broad Street and, at Christmastime, produced one of the best displays of seasonal fare seen in Banbury; Donald Gillies qualified as a doctor and for many years worked in London.

Where they stand was called hundred acre field and belonged to a Mr Denchfield. It stretched from the Oxford road to the Bloxham road and started to be covered by a tide of houses in the 1920s, becoming known as the Easington Estate.

Christine Bennett with others at Friday Badminton Club. Back row, left to right: Lillian Smith, Mrs Marjorie Brummett, –, Mrs H.O. Bennett, Mrs Davies, –, Mary Gardner. Sitting: Mrs Betts, Mrs Maycock, Mrs Salmon, Mrs Jelfs, Miss Bennett, Mrs Taylor. Centre: –, Marjorie Heynes.

High Street

The Cross area where the upper High Street meets the Horse Fair has been the scene of many notable occasions.

If the man who has raised his hat is any guide, the chauffeur-driven car holds a special visitor to Banbury, possibly a royal person. Behind those waiting on the pavement are the premises of traders who were part of the 1930s town.

The garage belonged to Sidney Ewins whose civic life culminated in a mayoral period. Next to his enterprise was a popular shoe repair business belonging to Harriss and Son. Just in frame is where Joe Bustin conducted his electrical engineering business. Joe had a car fit for a king and on more than one occasion he drove Edward VII from Banbury railway station to Broughton Castle.

Sidney Ewins in his mayoral year.

Like the Red Lion and White Lion hotels, the White Horse was much frequented by people connected with Banbury's market role. In 1885, Mr Busby, the proprietor, developed a popular choice on the 'market ordinary' menu which was chops and steak from the grill.

The White Horse Hotel.

When the Hunt/Usher family acquired the White Horse in 1936, it was clear that the rear of the hotel had been little altered since Mr Busby's days. A walk through the central arch shown in the picture was a journey back into the past. There were stables with blue flag floors and a series of loose boxes set against the churchyard wall. Nearby was a cottage, probably originally for the groom, but in the 1930s it was occupied by a reclusive, elderly couple. He always sported a suit and she wore a black hat and button-up shoes. When out together he always walked in front of her.

In the early 1960s, members of the Banbury Historical Society under Roger Fearon excavated part of the White Lion site. They explored cellars which were ten feet deep and extended about ten yards from the street. It was presumed that these cellars dated from the 18th and 19th centuries. At the time of their 1962 report, members noted the discovery of some mediaeval pottery and also parts of the foundations of the hotel.

Elsewhere at the rear of the White Horse there was space for carriages under a tin roof, a billiard room and a long room for meetings in which was the insignia of the Banbury Harriers.

The hotel experience was a complete contrast for this Warwickshire family. Previously they had run the Kineton 'Green' Bus Company which had a route to Banbury, terminating in the Horse Fair. Unfortunately, a fire destroyed their garage and vehicles and they were encouraged by a friend to try the hotel business.

At the end of the nineteenth century, the building next door had plate glass windows. It was the shop of J.H. Shepherd who was a baker and confectioner for 45 years, and was also the first president of the Banbury Medical Friendly Society. Shepherd established the first ever restaurant in Banbury. Sadly his death occurred during a dinner at the White Horse in 1894.

J.H. Shepherd's shop.

Grooms enjoy a drink.

Family and public house are often linked in specific and fascinating ways. Number 39 High Street was called Gazey's Wine and Spirits Vaults in 1851. Gazey also had a retail outlet in nearby Calthorpe Street. With the advent of George Watson nine years later, business activities were consolidated in the High Street.

The Watson's house had a substantial garden which was the scene for a gathering of the Watson and Fortescue boys, circa 1890. The Fortescues were solicitors in the town.

The Watson and Fortescue boys.

Someone who knew the house in the 1920s was Kathleen Hemmings (née White). She and her friends from Miss Bromley's North Bar School used to play in the garden with its vine and fine summer houses.

Frank Watson and his wife made a great impression on Kathleen who saw Mrs Watson as a lady of means determined to live appropriately. The large house was run with the help of Lizzy, the cook, and Ella, the maid. Lizzy lived in Castle Street. There was also a nanny, Nurse Clifford, who lived in. She had worked in Merton Street and had a brother who lived in the same Grimsbury street.

Frank Watson and his son Geoff in the Wine Vaults.

Frank sold out to the Hunt/Usher family in 1944. The new owners re-vamped the wine vaults and then developed the Inn Within. It offered a range of snacks as a prelude to events.

An advertisement fot The Inn Within.

The indoor bowling green at the Winter Gardens.

The Winter Gardens were fashioned out of the garden ground on which previously there had been a row of cottages and a lodging house dating back to about 1800. One of these cottages had been used by George Watson as a mushroom shed and amongst the notices on its door was one indicating how to dispose of bugs and lice.

When the excavations were started for the foundations of the Winter Gardens, 70 loads of earth a day for ten days were removed and distributed to the gardens of old and new houses around the town. It is said that these gardens gained in fertility.

The original gardens of the Watsons were enjoyed only by family and friends. By contrast, the Winter Gardens gave pleasure to countless numbers of people. Initially, as indicated by the Blinkhorn's picture, above, the only activity was indoor bowls. This choice of pursuit was conditioned by Charles Hunt's love of the game. However, it was not a financial success and diversification was clearly necessary. Dancing was part of the answer and in October 1956 the opening Ball took place.

Souvenir Programme

OPENING BALL
of the
WINTER GARDENS
BANBURY

OCTOBER 9th, 1956   -   -   -   9 p.m. - 2 a.m.

Superintendent Buckingham introduced the Hunts and Mrs. Usher who then declared the Winter Gardens open. Ken Prewer played, Pat Husselbee, Miss Banbury, was in attendance and there was a cabaret by the winners of the television programme 'Top Town' with Allan Course.

Between 1956 and 1982, many different forms of music were presented, ranging from strict tempo through jazz to the big beat sound. Top quality dance bands included the likes of Ted Heath, Joe Loss and Victor Sylvester. There were good local support groups, notably Brownie Lay.

Ethel Usher with Victor Sylvester, a reminder of the days when strict tempo dancing was highly popular at the Winter Gardens.

Very special occasions were the New Year's Eve dances. Just before midnight, some 400 hundred people would burst onto the High Street, conga up it and around the Cross and then 700 people would return to the Winter Gardens. Some 300 hundred lacked tickets but boosted the bar sales during the extended hours. Popular music and jazz evenings were major features. The Rolling Stones came twice but Ethel Usher turned down a prospective Beatles visit because the boys wanted £500, more than she had ever paid. Identifying who to invite from the pop scene was left to Charles Hunt, Jr, who watched the television programmes Top of the Pops and 6.5 Special to identify up and coming groups.

On the jazz front, Chris Barber and Acker Bilk with his Paramount Jazzmen were huge successes. These evenings were good for whisky sales! Boxing and wrestling supplied a complete contrast. Ethel became renowned as the only female boxing promoter in the country. Support for the wrestling came from near and far. There was always a hard core support including a farmer called Hemmings from the Wykham Lane area. These people would dash to the Inn Within at the end of bouts and book for the next time. Famous wrestlers such as Big Daddy and Giant Haystack were sometimes on the card but curiously it was often Banbury's very own Jack Pallow who got the crowd going. Other events in the Winter Gardens included trade shows, fashion parades, antique fairs and opportunities for roller skating.

Fashion Show at the Winter Gardens.

Skaters between the Winter Gardens and the Inn Within.

On top of all this, and in the days before the motorway with its service centre, tourists came in their droves for breakfast and lunch. Up to 700 at a time was not unknown.

1982 saw the end to this amazing whirl of activities. Ethel Usher will forever be remembered as Banbury's impressario. She tried to find a new owner willing to don the mantle but in the end had to sell, knowing that redevelopment was round the corner and Banbury had lost an institution.

Banbury Post Office about 1930.

Postal services moved from Parsons Street to the building in the picture during 1849. Originally, there was a double set of steps leading up to the entrance. Reconstructions of the premises took place in 1911 and 1936. Part of the plan at the earlier date was to convert a rear garden into a covered yard for mail vans and carts with access from Church Passage ('Tink-a-Tank').

At the junction of the High Street and Calthorpe Street H. B. Stanley had a book-setting business from 1852. He stocked Wilson's views of Banbury and district and acted as the receiver for luggage belonging to passengers using the trains which operated in and out of Merton Street.

Stanleys' shop on High Street decorated for Queen Victorias Diamond Jubilee in 1897.

S. & H. Jones
and Co.

One of the few family businesses left in Banbury is S. H. Jones & Co., wine merchants, who had moved from earlier premises in the Horse Fair in 1901. Their fine sixteenth century building includes a massive chimney breast, a reminder of the day when the building was a bakery.

The right-hand side of the same picture shows a view looking down Marlborough Road to the Wesleyan Methodist Church. In 1863, when Dr. Stanton Wise was developing his Beech Lawn Estate, Marlborough Road was cut through from Newlands to the High Street.

HIGH STREET, BANBURY—PROPRIETOR: W. J. PULLEN

For the young who want smartness without extravagance

On the opposite side of the road, just before the White Lion, was Judges, still dear to many Banbury hearts. The shop was so popular that people using the B5 bus service from Bretch Hill always asked for Judges long after it was replaced by Curry's electrical.

deréta

Spring time . . , Pure wool in pastels . . . piquant shoulders cut in one with the yoke . . . deep roomy pockets . . . buttons in gay twin rows.

£7.3.7

A 1947 advertisement.

Judges shop window.

A coach typical of those using the White Lion.

The White Lion was probably Banbury's best known coaching inn. According to Rusher's 1837 Directory and list, Royal Mail services left for London every night and for Birmingham each morning.

A brochure and tariff for 1909 gives the proprietor as T.A. Page. He participated in local affairs, including the Banbury Steeplechases for which he was the starter.

A prominant feature of the inn yard still surviving is the lovely wisteria claimed to be over 200 years old.

The White Lion yard and wisteria.

Many important gatherings took place on the premises. In this picture, taken in 1909, people are eager to get a sight of the colonial editors. In their midst would have been Randolph Webb of the *Banbury Advertiser.*

The colonial editors at Banbury.

The Red Lion and High Street.

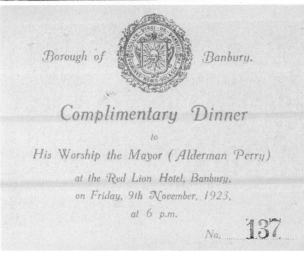

The Red Lion was very popular with farmers when they came into Banbury for the Thursday market. It was also a well-known venue for dinners such as the Corporation Dinner of 1923 when Alderman Perry was mayor.

A third, and contrasting, use of the hotel was for sales, such as the 1920 Lampet estate disposal. There were over 750 acres of farmland and associated property.

In the early 1930s, the Red Lion was pulled down to make way for F.W. Woolworth.

F.W. Woolworth.

Woolworths had the same reputation as the first Tesco supermarkets — stack it high and sell it cheap. In the 1930s, it was called the 3d and 6d store, reflecting the prices charged. Many people like Violet Beale and Dorothy Franklin were attracted to spend the whole day savouring the delights of the counters. Shop assistants had to be raised up by platforms to see across these. Rhoda Woodward of Adderbury saw the coming of Woolworths as a retail revolution. The uniqueness meant huge crowds in the shop on market days and there was the great attraction of the milk bar.

Vivers Building occupied, in part, by Neale and Perkins.

Clearly visible near the cart is the Vivers building. Edward Vivers was a wealthy cloth merchant in the seventeenth century and his house has at various times been occupied by the makers of the Banbury Cake, notably Alfred Betts.

Adjoining Betts shop was that established by Messrs. Neale and Perkins. They were ironmongers but, unlike many of their competitors, their goods appealed more to people such as farmers' wives rather than the farmers themselves. A classic case was the lady who bought a tin kettle for 6d. When that developed a hole she was able to get it repaired by Neale and Perkins who charged her a further 6d.

In the 1890s, Joseph Perkins extended his activities to include the making of copper items for the big houses in the Banbury region. These were produced at his workshop in Pepper Alley. In 1909, Norman White took over management of the shop in the High Street. He was a Banbury man having been the first person to be born in Albert Street. Like so many other retailers of the earlier years of this century, he lived above the shop.

CARPETS FOR 1932

Modern Designs

Eastern Reproductions

Small Damask Effects

Quite Plain Colours

Now being shown

at

High St. & Broad St. • BANBURY

Left: an elegant lady is a respected customer at Chapmans.
Above: Edgar Chapman.

Chapmans became one of the best known retail companies in Banbury. Their furniture and fittings business together with a removal service had traded out of 2 High Street since just before the turn of the century. A prime mover in the business was Edgar Chapman.

Most people in Banbury will remember the company on the Northern side of Bridge Street, but an intermediate location was on the southern facade in place of Allsopps.

Telephone—P.O. 18   Established 100 years

Roasting Coffee 1632

Ernest Butler

Tea and Coffee Specialist

High Street : Banbury

An advertisement
for Butlers.

Butlers, also in the lower High Street and near Pepper Alley, was a popular grocery store and rivals of Dossetts in Parsons Street.

Ernest Butler took over No. 4 in 1901. As the advertisement indicates, his business was symbolised by coffee roasting. The nearby High Street often had black smoke from this process.

Bob Green was apprenticed at Butlers in the 1930s. He was expected to sample all aspects of the business. In the shop this meant weighing, preparing commodities and servicing at the counter. As Butlers derived much trade from the surrounding villages, work also included several bicycle rides each week to secure orders and be back at the shop by 4.00 p.m. so that these could be got ready for despatch by van. A typical run was to Hook Norton and Sibfords via Wroxton and Shutford. If time permitted, some lunch was taken at the Lampet Arms. Villages were not visited on Thursday because of Market Day pressures at Butlers shop. Town orders were collected every Friday. Hours of work were significantly different from firms like Hoods. Butlers closed at 5.30 p.m. Monday to Friday but remained open on Saturday to at least 8.00 p.m. and even later if other shops were still trading. They closed half-day on Tuesday.

Postscript

A significant sociological study of Banbury was *Tradition and Change* by Margaret Stacey, published in 1960. It perceived differences between Banburians and aliens or outsiders. In a way, this recognised the movement of the town from a family and market oriented place to somewhere increasingly dominated by industry and commerce, especially on the fringes, and controlled from outside Banbury.

Margaret's vision of the pre-1930 town with its carriers carts, steaming cattle and noisy drovers equates with Banburyness in those who recall those characteristics.

As this book has demonstrated, remembered Banbury was also a place of lively and well-loved family businesses. Living above their shops meant commitment to specific parts of the town centre. Each street scene was different yet still a combination of butcher, baker and candlestick maker.

Progressively from about 1970 onwards, the decline of the nineteenth century Cherwell district, regulations governing traffic, including buses, and the arrival of a town centre shopping mall, have resulted in new patterns of retailing in the traditional shopping streets. The present High Street has no butcher yet several card shops.

Even the produce market is less vibrant than in the days of Rocky Leach. Cakes, crosses and cattle created a different environment from that of today. Despite increased mobility and more tenuous allegiances, a new generation of Banburians needs to respond to the question, 'What kind of a town do you want?'